# Personal Branding Blueprints

## 27 of My Best Marketing Notes You Can Use to Build Your Influence, Grow Your Business, and Get More Referrals

### TIM DAVIS

Founder and Creator of Personal Branding Mastery Seminars and AgentMarketingAcademy.com

Published by Marketing Evangelist Publishing

REACH THE AUTHOR AND ORDER MORE COPIES AT:

www.PersonalBrandingMastery.com

TimDavisOnline@me.com

Printed in the United States of America

ISBN-13: 978-1537071787

ISBN-10: 1537071785

# Real Stories from Agents Just Like You!

"I was hesitant about branding. I didn't want to come across as a bragger, but working with Tim changed my thinking. In fact, Lucy and I started serving new clients almost instantly as a result of the branding strategies we learned!
Beverly Jones and Lucy, Nashville, TN

# Even More Real Stories from Agents Just Like You!

**"I have been a broker for over 20 years and I thought I had seen it all when it comes to marketing. I reluctantly went to the event planning to slip out the back door as soon as I could. I stayed the entire time and took pages of notes!"**
**Dale Irwin, Keller Williams Fort Worth Tx**

# Even More Real Stories from Agents Just Like You!

"Agents get invited to a ton of events and so many of them under deliver value, but not Personal Branding Mastery! I now know exactly step by step what to do to build my brand. Tons of value and real action plans!
Dee Matthews, Keller Williams Plano Texas

# Even More Real Stories from Agents Just Like You!

"The content was robust, brilliant, and I was thoroughly impressed. In fact I had 3 deals closing the day of the event but I stayed the whole time because the content was critical to my business!
Amber Noble Garland, KW, Morganville, Nj

# Even More Real Stories from Agents Just Like You!

"I only follow the best leaders like Seth Godin, Gary Vee, and Tim Davis. I drove 2 hours one way just to go to the Personal Branding Mastery Event! Best decision period!
Dan Weis, Comey & Sheppard, Cincinnati

TIM DAVIS

STOP NEGOTIATING **WITH** YOUR GOALS. SET THEM AND PAY THE PRICE!

BuildYourBrandNow

# A Personal Note from Me to You

You are stronger than you think, bigger than your fears and designed to overcome your doubts. Inside you are gifts and talents that were intentionally placed there for you to develop, grow and unleash to serve others.

Nothing could be worse than to deny those gifts, allow them to lay dormant and quietly slip away. Right now is the time to begin the investment in yourself to become the person you were designed to be.

Screw that voice which attempts to derail you from the purpose for your life. Stand up, be strong, look the fear right in the eye and go for it afraid.

# ACKNOWLEDGMENTS

Thank you to all my friends on and off social media. You have followed my rants for years and you make life more fun! I enjoy connecting with you everyday and seeing your adventures. Keep growing, hustling, and grinding it out towards your dreams!

SUCCESS REQUIRES
YOU TO HUSTLE,
GRIND AND
REPEAT
BuildYourBrandNow

We always had more month than money when I was growing up. My father passed away when I was only three years old. My mom and I lived in the projects and received welfare. Although my mother did the best she could, there were many days where she was so drugged out on prescription medication she spent the day in bed. I had to learn how to entertain and take care of myself.

Over time, I began to observe people. I noticed that not everyone lived in the projects. I noticed my friends had homes, their parents had jobs and money. As a result, they had opportunities I did not.

When I turned 16, I began working at a local grocery store about two and a half miles from our apartment. The brown Pontiac Lemans car we owned wasn't reliable, so there were many days I walked to and from work. I never minded the walk because my focus was on the result…we needed money to live. Life is that way. You will need to do things you don't like. The truth is that if you keep your eye on the result, you won't mind the work.

I learned a major life lesson from Mr. Smith, the owner of Smith's Grocery. He shared with me on my first day that I must be more valuable to them than the job was to me. He could, at any time, find my replacement. In other words, I must prove myself every day, on every shift.

My first goal was to get a promotion from the back room, where I washed and sorted the returned glass Coke bottles, to stocker and bagger. I promise you that no one sorted bottles and kept a better back room than me. I was determined to bring value. You must become determined to succeed also.

The lessons I learned at Smith's grocery, combined with the skill I developed of observation are the beginning foundations of what is now Personal Branding Mastery. I am still learning, still growing, and still adding to PBM, but in this book, you will discover core strategies that will elevate your level of influence.

Above everything, remember this…You and I must ALWAYS be more valuable to the market than they are to us. The instant we stop bringing value, we will be replaced…no questions asked.

That being said, let's get started.

A 2013 Gallup poll survey asked consumers one question…

"Do you trust real estate agents?"

67.5% people responded NO; they do not trust agents. When you break down the responses into age categories, consumers between 18-35 had a 72.5% negative response. If you think about that for a minute, 7 out of every 10 people under the age of 35 said they do not trust real estate agents. How could this possibly be? The majority of this age group has yet to buy or sell real estate?

Some of the topics we will discuss in this book may be hard to hear at first. I don't say them to make you feel bad. It is just the opposite. I care about your success. I know you have hopes, dreams, and goals. I believe that you want to be successful. That is why we must address reality. You and I must work hard to change the perception so many have of the profession.

We must agree that the majority of people have formed a negative opinion about agents, and we need to discover how this happens. The majority portion of their bias is driven by the media. AT&T Wireless ran a national TV commercial that portrayed agents as older, out of touch, busy, arrogant people who were rather bossy. One fact about influence is that the media, especially television, controls a majority of people's opinions.

Another contributing factor is that certain industries have a "black-eye" reputation. Take the auto sales business as an example. Would you be open to a conversation with a person who introduced themselves as a used car salesman? I am going to guess that you would be hesitant at best. Another example would be Multi-Level Networking. Many people put this business in the negative perception category. We discuss "black-eye" perception on our Personal Branding Mastery podcast. You can subscribe to the podcast on iTunes for free at PersonalBrandingMasteryPodcast.com

Real estate just happens also to be in the "black-eye" category. Regardless of why or how this has occurred, you and I must subscribe to the foundational principle that perception is reality.

My promise to you is…strategies you find inside this book, on our website and our podcast are real strategies that we have used to build our business and business of agents. Personal Branding is not theory or wishful thinking. Our marketing is on the ground, in the trenches, real-world plans that produce results.

I know first hand what it is like to feel as if I was a better choice for the client, only to have them choose my competitor over me. I can't blame the prospect. For me to get better, I had to point the finger at myself. What did I not know that would have made the difference? How could I improve my brand, my message, the client experience and a whole host of other parts of the business to end this cycle of losing customers?

I walked through the fire of rejection and spent countless nights studying, refining and perfecting my brand. What I learned is contained in this book. It is yours to use but understand this truth…your brand is built over time, not overnight. You must put in the work. A personal brand is just that…it is personal. That means it requires YOU to get your hands dirty wrestling with the process.

I know too many people who want a quick fix. They want to avoid the process because the process takes time. Growth is painful, consuming and expensive. It requires you to invest your time, energy, and money. You will need to turn off Dancing with the Stars and do the hard work of building your brand. You must get honest with yourself and get honest with the universal truths of marketing and influence. You will need to learn and acquire new skills.

For example, when I began building my brand, I knew nothing about publishing a book, recording a podcast, creating an infographic and more. I had to learn these skills and learning takes time. I had to skin my knee, get knocked down, fail and then get back up. You will too.

I had to work to find my voice…so will you. I had to endure critics…so will you. I had to fight back self-doubt…so will you. I had to change my thinking…so will you.

You may not "feel" ready. You may be afraid…but you MUST start right now…afraid. Time waits for no one.

At this very moment, you have a personal brand. You may not have been intentional about creating or designing it, but you have one none the less. The reason you have a brand is that people do judge a book by its cover. People make decisions and place labels on others. They make judgment calls regarding your level of success, competence, and skills.

If you disregard intentionally creating your brand, then the market will attach a label to you and their label may or may not be the one you want.

ALWAYS ENSURE THAT YOU PUT PEOPLE AHEAD OF PROFITS

BuildYourBrandNow

I remember the story like it was yesterday. My team and I had been working to get a mortgage loan approved for a client. The transaction was exceptionally difficult to put together. There were times that it looked like the deal was on life support, but this family desperately wanted to purchase their first home.

As we worked through the file we discovered that the home value was slightly less than anticipated. For us to make this deal work, we decided to forego our fees and commissions. Because of our relationship with our title company they also agreed to give up their earnings, but we were still short. The young couple was strapped for cash. They had exhausted all of their avenues to make the deal work. The last place to turn were the agents.

I thought this would be no problem. The deal only needed $1000 to come together. Who wouldn't agree to give a $1000 credit? I was in for a big surprise.

When we asked the agents to help everyone out with a $1000 credit, they each declined. What? How could that be? They were willing to let this young couple miss out because of $1000. Everyone else had given, but they refused and the loan never closed. It was a case of profits before people.

Trust me when I say this…you will NEVER and I mean NEVER lose when you put people ahead of profits. People matter. Help them. Be their advocate. You will reap tremendous rewards when you do.

BECOME KNOWN AS THE AGENT WHO DELIVERS THE RESULTS

BuildYourBrandNow

Each of your buyers and sellers wants one thing…**results**. Your job is to become known to your ideal client for delivering the results they want…nothing less. When real estate conversations start, you want your name to be the only name passed around because you are known for delivering results.

How do you identify what your ideal customer want? First, you must clearly identify your ideal client. Get specific and focus on a niche.

Who are they? Where do they live? What type of work do they do? How old are they? Once you determine your ideal client, you will want to spend time considering what it is like to walk a mile in their shoes. You can begin by interviewing people who match your **Ideal Client Profile™** and ask them…what do they want when it comes to buying your selling. Their answers then become your brand message. Here is my formula…

I work with ____(niche market)____ who want ____(their answers) so they can achieve ____(significant result)____

As you get results for your clients, make the results the focal point of your message. It is time to step away from your production claims and start focusing on the results your customers achieve.

DEVELOP THE IMAGE OF THE PERSON YOU WANT TO BECOME

BuildYourBrandNow

What is your current self-image? Who is the person you want to become? What do you want to be known for in the community?

An essential part of building your personal brand is capturing a vision and image of the person you want to become. The Bible says in Proverbs 29:18, "where there is no vision the people perish…" If you believe you will become the number one choice in real estate for your ideal client, over time you will take the necessary action steps to become that agent.

*"Our self-image, strongly held, essentially determines what we become."* — *Maxwell Maltz*

The first step to developing your self-image is to identify successful agents and other professionals that you admire. I prefer to make a list of industry thought leaders. Once you have your list, ask yourself these questions…

1.  What do I admire about them?
2.  How do they dress, talk and act?
3.  What qualities do they have that inspire you?
4.  What do you need to do to be the best version of you?

From there, you will want to identify where you are now and how you intend to invest in your personal and professional growth.

DETERMINE YOUR IDEAL CUSTOMER THAT YOU LOVE TO SERVE

BuildYourBrandNow

When I was getting started, I believed that anyone needing a mortgage loan was my client. I had no defined message and so I attracted anyone and everyone. Over time this method became exhausting.

*"Remember you can't please everyone, but you can make a life-changing difference for someone. Find them and serve them!"*

This lead to multiple problems in my business. We were inconsistent, and customer service levels were not where they needed to be. I needed a solution and the solution was to clearly define a niche market.

Here is the method I used to define my **Ideal Client Profile™.** If you follow these two steps, you will identify your ideal client.

1. I made a list of my favorite clients. The ones who were my advocates. The customers who we loved and they loved how we served them.
2. I began to look for what they had in common. This included their careers, their attitudes, and their wants

What I discovered was that my ideal client was someone who was self-employed. I loved working with them and they loved us. Immediately I began to market our business to customers who were self-employed. This allowed us to create a **Client Attraction Message™**, identify the first responders (like CPA's and financial planners) who already knew them, and develop systems to create a **Total Client Experience™**

**DEVELOP YOUR BRAND IMAGE THAT MATCHES YOU AND YOUR TARGET MARKET**

BuildYourBrandNow

!

There is an old saying that says, "if you want to attract the squirrel, you must look like the squirrel." I live in Nashville, Tennessee, and when I began working with self-employed clients I met a CPA, Clyde Bright. His main focus was on customers in the music industry. We were able to serve several high profile music artist over the years. What I found was that if I wore a suit and tie to those meetings, the clients felt uneasy. These were music artist and they felt more comfortable when my image most resembled theirs.

One year the city commissioned a statue on music row. It was an enormous bronze statue of naked men and women. It was controversial, to say the least, but on music row, it was accepted. I took a picture of the statue and added myself and my team's heads on the figures. I then created a flyer that said; "You write the songs, we write the mortgage loans!"

The music industry loved it. I went on to define the clothing I would wear, the professional pictures I had made and the colors of our logo and business. It all matters. Remember, **perception is reality,** and you are in control of the perception. You must decide for yourself what you want your image to be. Invest in your pictures. Invest in your wardrobe. Invest in your graphic design because you never know when your first impression will occur. Always be prepared to make the impression you want. We live in a social media driven world, so remember what you post online counts too!

DEVELOP A RESULTS MESSAGE BASED FOR WHAT YOUR CLIENTS WANT AND WHY

BuildYourBrandNow

When you go to create your **Client Attraction Message™**, remember that people will reluctantly buy what they need, but they will have a yard sale to get what they want. The key here is in the word want. When you use the word "need", people build a wall, but when you use the word want, they lean in.

The formula I use is this…

What does your ideal client want? What will they achieve for getting what they want? What do they gain as a result of buying a home?

When I was serving self-employed clients, I once worked with a prominent record executive. This music producer purchased a million dollar home, but the real reason behind his purchase was so that he could entertain music artist he wanted to sign to his record label.

Feel free to use this formula for your real estate business…

I work with **(insert your ideal client)** who want **(affordable homes, luxury real estate, whatever you discover they want)** so they can **(the big result they achieve)**

BECAUSE FACTS TELL AND STORIES SELL REFINE YOUR BRAND STORY

BuildYourBrandNow

Stories are the backbone of life. We have been telling and passing down stories from generation to generation since the beginning of time. The art of "story-telling" is a craft you can and must learn. You begin with your story. Your personal life story reveals clues for connection with your market.

I want you to think about the relationships you have in life that mean the most to you. Outside of your family, did those relationships begin because of business or because of connection?

Your personal brand should contain two stories. Your story to create connection and your clients stories to generate referrals. Here is how you can define your story.

What has happened in your life that has made you who you are?
What are the lessons you have learned along the way that you want others to know?
What do you love?
What are your hobbies and interest?
What are five things no one knows about you?

When you take the time to tell your story, you will find it connects with people on a deeper level than just preaching to them about your business. I have a friend who loves restaurants. He has combined his love for food with real estate and now he creates Real Estate and Restaurant videos where he features local business and talks real estate. Bottom line…Video is a powerful way to brand yourself.

PULL
TOGETHER
TESTIMONIALS
FROM
YOUR
BRAND
ADVOCATES
BuildYourBrandNow

Have you every seen a really great movie that you couldn't wait to tell everyone about? How about a restaurant or event? We have all had an experience that we wanted to share with others. That is the power of testimonials. What someone else says about your brand is much more powerful than what you say about yourself.

**We have a FREE resource for you…The Ultimate Testimonial Toolkit**

## How to Collect & Share 5-Star Rave Reviews on Autopilot (While You Sleep)... In this informative 24-page guide, you'll learn the insider secrets for turning your clients into raving fan evangelists and supercharging your client attraction at the *SPEED* of *TRUST*. 100% free!

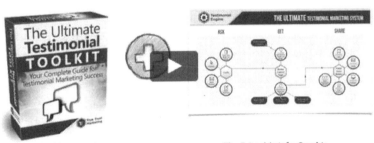

Go to www.PersonalBrandingTestimonialToolkit.com to get your free guide!

BE PREPARED TO
FIGHT BACK
SELF
DOUBT
AND CRITICS
BuildYourBrandNow

I believe we each have a voice. Too many people suppress their voice because they fear what other people may say or think. The reality is that no of us can please everyone. Someone is always going to have an opinion. The key is to let your real, authentic voice out.

Think about some very polarizing people like Howard Stern, Donald Trump, Dave Ramsey and others. Does everyone like them? NO! Do they worry about suppressing their voice because of critics? NO! They have strong beliefs and convictions. They preach their message and the critics complain, but the tribe of people who love them, listen to the message and join in.

Think about these questions…

- What do you believe?
- Do you often suppress your authentic voice to please everyone?
- What would happen if you unleashed your true self?
- How would you feel?
- Would you be more productive?
- Are you willing to fight the self-doubt and be yourself?

CREATE YOUR
PERSONAL
BRAND IDENTITY
NAME
BuildYourBrandNow

For as long as I can remember I have struggled to remember people's names. I wonder if you can relate? I began to think that if I had trouble remembering names, maybe other people struggled with this as well. I talked to hundreds of business professionals who admitted they had problems with names too. During my research, I discovered that celebrities (both local and national) rarely went by their name. Instead, they created a character name.

Take Dwayne Johnson for example. He is best known as "The Rock". William Shatner is another example. He is currently known as "The Priceline Negotiator". And finally, look at Cesar Millan. His character name is "The Dog Whisperer".

I took a clue from these celebrities about names and began to call myself The Mortgage Evangelist. When I moved into coaching and training, I adapted the name to become The Marketing Evangelist. What I discovered was that people remembered the character name. It made it easier for them to find me online as well.

Creating a character name, like Jonathan Andrews who is known as, The New Home Negotiator, can go a long way in building your brand. You must own it, but when you do, you will discover that more clients will remember you and send you more referrals!

SECURE YOUR BRAND IDENTITY ACROSS THE MAJOR SOCIAL MEDIA CHANNELS

BuildYourBrandNow

Social media is too powerful to ignore. Once you have created your character name, you must make sure you can secure it across various social media platforms even if you don't currently use them.

Let's say you decided to specialize in working with physicians. You choose to name yourself The Real Estate Doctor. Before you become married to that name, make sure you can lock it down on these platforms...

☐ Facebook Business Page
☐ Twitter
☐ Instagram
☐ YouTube
☐ Pinterest
☐ LinkedIN
☐ SnapChat
☐ Tumblr

Remember, you may not be using all of these channels, but go ahead and secure the name. As your business grows, you can add content to the channels you choose and where your target market is searching.

BUILD YOUR VISUAL
STEP BY STEP SYSTEM THAT DELIVERS RESULTS

BuildYourBrandNow

I always ask this question in my Personal Branding Mastery Seminars…Do you have the same contracts, process, and MLS that other agents have? The chances are 100% that your answer is YES. If everything is the same, then what makes you different?

The answer is in creating your own unique selling system. If you write out the steps you take to help someone buy or sell a home, you will find it is just like every other agent…BUT…

If you give your system a **name** and an **infographic**, then you can move from being the same to standing out.

Here is what I mean…

If you are serving the first time buyer market in Donelson, TN (or your city), then you could create The Donelson Tennessee First Time Buyer Blueprint. By just adding a name to your system, you will create a powerful point of separation. Product and system naming is a simple strategy that can be very powerful in building your brand and attracting more clients.

GET QUOTED IN THE MEDIA AS THE ADVOCATE AND TRUSTED SOURCE FOR YOUR MARKET

BuildYourBrandNow

Barbara Corcoran of the hit TV show Shark Tank was once a struggling real estate broker on the verge of collapse. She tells the story of how she created a simple report on rents and values of real estate in the New York market. She named her report, "The Corcoran Report" (remember to title your information to make it unique) and it was picked up by The Wall Street Journal. Her business began to turn around almost immediately. She had discovered the power of being quoted in the media.

She has since gone on to say, "if you are regularly quoted in the media as an expert in your field, people will believe you are." That is why I put together a program where you can be quoted in the affiliate news stations of major media outlets such as ABC, NBC, CBS, and FOX. In my program, you can write and submit one story per month, and we will get it published in the media.

The media is the number one influencer of public opinion. Maybe you have been in a situation where the news came out with an unfavorable story about the real estate market. The next day you were forced to overcome a ton of objections from clients because they "heard on the news" that the real estate market was not good. It's time you fought that battle on the same front. Now you can with the ability to get on the news with our monthly media promotion package. Email me at timdavisonline@me.com or visit PersonalBrandingMastery.com to find out more.

BEGIN PUBLISHING EDUCATIONAL CONTENT THAT POSITIONS YOU AS THE EDUCATOR AND ADVOCATE

BuildYourBrandNow

We live in a unique time. You and I can publish content that was once only reserved for people who had the right connections. In the past, you needed to know someone in TV, radio, and publishing. That is no longer the case. You and I can start our own online magazine in a weekend. You smartphone holds the power of a complete video studio in your hand.

The key is to publish content that positions yourself as the educator and advocate for your market. Take a look at Dave Ramsey. He is on the radio talking about personal finance. His show leads to other opportunities for his business. You can do the same thing in your business. Educate first, sell later.

Here are five ways to publish information that will elevate your influence…

1. Blogs
2. Videos
3. Podcast
4. News Papers
5. Books

The key is not to get caught up in being perfect. Just get started and get better along the way.

PUBLISH A BOOK THAT
SOLVES YOUR CLIENTS
PROBLEMS
BuildYourBrandNow

In our Personal Branding Mastery Seminars, I reveal how powerful having your own published book can be for your business. It is far and away the number one tool in building your brand authority.

Michael Hyatt, the former CEO of Thomas nelson Publishing, says that having your own published book will

- Establish you immediately as the authority
- Build more credibility for you in the market
- Instantly increase your influence
- Immediately increase conversions
- Build a trust bridge between yourself and your target market
- Increase your sales

My good friend Monte Mohr who's real estate team will sell close to 500 homes in 2016 has his own book. In fact, he has written and published two books. One of his team members shared with me that the book is the number one conversion tool they have in their arsenal.

If you want to publish your own book, visit PersonalBrandingMastery.com or email me at timdavisonline@me.com

DEVELOP YOUR PRESENTATION SKILLS AND BECOME KNOWN AS A SPEAKER

BuildYourBrandNow

One of the biggest fears people have is the fear of public speaking. Because so many people fear public speaking, it can go a long way in establishing your brand authority if you start speaking to groups. As a real estate professional, you could develop three to five presentations that could be given to local organizations in your community.

Real estate is always a hot topic in any market. If the market is good, then your presentations can center around how to win in a hot market. If the market has cooled, you can use that same presentation in reverse. When you speak, you are not only increasing your influence but you are also leveraging your time.

If you spoke in font of 75 professionals at the Chamber of Commerce, you would be touching 75 people in one hour versus one to one which could add up to 75 hours or more. I call this a "one to many" approach. It requires you to get outside of your comfort zone, but the returns are fantastic. Here is a short list of places you could speak in your community

- Chambers of Commerce
- Local Meet Up Groups
- Networking Events
- Associations
- Rotary Clubs and organizations

ALIGN YOURSELF WITH A CHARITY CLOSE TO YOUR HEART AND GIVE BACK

BuildYourBrandNow

Hopefully, you are not in business to only build your empire and nothing else. We each gain much more from life when we seek to give first. Years ago, I began working with a local charity called Happy Tails Humane. I have a deep passion for animals, especially dogs. Happy Tails is a local no-kill animal shelter that will work to find a permanent home for abandoned and stray animals.

We have three dogs now, but at the time, we owned two. Quincy and Fudge were our cocker spaniels, and we partnered with Happy Tails to donate a portion of every closing to their organization. It was an incredible partnership. They even added posters of us in their shelter. We added personal flyers of our dogs to each mortgage package so that our customers knew that by choosing us, they were also participating in a bigger mission.

They key to giving back is to find the charity you are passionate about serving. One of my friends, Beverly Jones, partners with Make a Wish. Another friend, Jonathan Romero, works with the Levine Cancer Institute and another friend works with Wesley House. They are each participating in growing their communities and giving back in a tangible way.

What are you passionate about? How could you strike up a partnership with a local charity? **Email me the charity you are going to start helping. I want to know. My email is timdavisonline@me.com**

WRITE AND PUBLISH ARTICLES FOR INDUSTRY BLOGS AND MAGAZINES

BuildYourBrandNow

After you have started publishing local information, you may want to reach out to industry blogs and magazines. They are constantly looking for writers to contribute content. By establishing yourself as a national writer on the subject of real estate, you can use their credibility in your local market. Imagine being able to share a national article you wrote with your local clients. You would be able to increase your credibility instantly.

The process of getting published nationally is easier than most people believe. If you gather up industry publications, you will find a page that list the editors of the magazine. On that page you, will find an email address where they are soliciting writers to submit articles for publication.

Once you have an article published, the majority of magazines will allow you to purchase reprints of your article. You can use the copies in your local marketing to increase your influence. An additional benefit is that you can use (with permission) their logo in your marketing. For example, you could say "as seen in" …XYZ publication.

Blogs are just a bit different. Some blogs will solicit for writers while others will require you to start a relationship with the blog owner. Either way, your brand can be well served by getting published on a national basis.

DEVELOP AND
HOST YOUR
OWN EVENT
FUNDRAISER
BuildYourBrandNow

When you couple your charitable giving with a local fund-raiser you will elevate your brand to a whole new level. Imagine that you have a love for raising money for cancer research. What would happen if you were the creator and founder of Your City's Run for Cancer where you combined your passion for running with your desire to raise money for cancer?

When you establish fund-raisers, you can connect with other influential people in your city like government officials, owners, executives of companies, and local influencers. They understand the power of giving back and will rally around your cause to help spread the word.

The questions you must answer are…

1. What are you passionate about?
2. What charity could use your support?
3. What type of annual event could you create?
4. Who will you need on your team to make it possible?

The key is to get started. Don't hesitate because my favorite quote is "Success favors speed of implementation."

CREATE AN
INVENTORY OF
SHOCK AND AWE
PACKAGES

BuildYourBrandNow

Have you ever been in a situation where you were a potential client told you that they were interviewing multiple agents? It is all too common because prospects today have a difficult time distinguishing between agents. Remember, customers are only looking for one thing…RESULTS!

We would mail our prospects what I call a Shock and Awe package. It was a box full of testimonials, an audio CD, a copy of our book and other educational information. We packed all of this in a box and sent it out to our prospects. This package was a real game changer. No one else was doing anything similar in the market, so we stood out head and shoulders above the competition.

The key to building your brand is to show up like nobody else. The best agents do not always win the deal…the best marketer does.

You don't need everything I mentioned above to start your package. You can begin with a few testimonials and a published article or two. Over time you can add more content to your shock and awe kit.

If you want to take it over the top? Send your package to where they work with some balloons. This way all of their co-workers will see it as well.

PUBLISH YOUR OWN
AUTHORITY CONNECTION NEWSLETTER
BuildYourBrandNow

The more technology becomes a part of our lives, the more I see people overlook the power of the mailbox. A well thought out newsletter will cause your brand to stand out and create a deeper bond with your customers. When you think about a newsletter, dismiss the typical thoughts of recipes and real estate articles. People crave connection. Make your newsletter stand out by sharing what makes up your life.

Every year we get Christmas cards, but only one person sends us a letter. That letter recaps their entire year from vacations to broken bones. I thoroughly enjoy receiving their letter because it makes me feel a deeper connection. I want you to think of your newsletter in the same way. For example, you know I am a dog lover. I may include a column from the dog's point of view. Tricks they have learned or shoes they may have eaten.

The key is to make your content engaging. You accomplish this when you open up and become more transparent.

What do you love?
What are some funny things that happen in your life?

Questions like these are where you begin.

DEVELOP A WORLD CLASS CLIENT EXPERIENCE THEY WILL NEVER FORGET

BuildYourBrandNow

Have you ever visited a department store like JC Penny? Have you ever been in a store like Nordstrom's? You will have two completely different experiences. The question becomes… "What is your client's experience like when they work with you?" have you designed a world class experience that makes them want to refer you all of their friends and family?

I planned out my entire client's experience from the time we first made contact, through the process, at closing and after. We had systems and marketing messages at each step.

I called the plan **Four Part Marketing™**. The Shock and Awe Package started the relationship. Once they became a client we sent gifts to where they worked. During the process, we had multiple communication touch points and a mailer that went to their home. At closing, we developed the Perfect Closing Gift. After closing, we enrolled them in our "post-closing client concierge plan". When we said clients for life, we meant every word.

My friend Aaron Ludin is an expert at client gifts. He makes real estate agents stand out, look great, and obtain more referrals. **Aaron says the lifetime value of a customer is $45,000! WOW!! They deserve a great gift at closing. Aaron is the owner of the Orlando Branding Agency and you need to give him a call at 407-720-TOMA.**

START AND HOST A LOCAL COMMUNITY PODCAST

BuildYourBrandNow

Podcasting began many years ago but is starting to gain serious momentum. I ran across the concept in 2008. I started a podcast on BlogTalkRadio.com called More Buyers and Sellers. What I liked about the format was that it was free. I had to deal with some commercials they played, but free is a good thing. What I liked about podcasting, was that after we had recorded an episode, it was automatically pushed out to iTunes. Now our little local show was available on iTunes. I could say "as heard on iTunes" in our marketing.

Podcasting has come a long way since 2008, but it is still a vast open market. You could use a service like BlogTalkRadio.com or pay a service like Libsyn.com to host your content. One has ads, the other doesn't, but both will push your content out to iTunes and other music hosting services.

We have a podcast called Personal Branding Mastery. You can listen on iTunes, Stitcher Radio, and Google Play. If you want to subscribe for free, type in PersonalBrandingMasteryPodcast.com

If I were selling real estate today, I would start a local business podcast. I would invite local business owners, executives and CEO's on to talk about their business. By giving them exposure, I would meet a ton of influential people and expand my influence. When you intentionally grow your network with people of influence, your business will grow in turn.

BUILD AND
ADMINISTER
ONLINE COMMUNITY
BuildYourBrandNow

Some days it seems like there is no end to the power of Facebook. You can build a brand incredibly fast using Facebook. One of the best methods is by creating a local community page. There is a local community forum on Facebook where I live called Hip Donelson. This one community has over 25,000 members. What would happen to your business if you were the page owner of a community with that many members?

Nothing is stopping you from creating your own community page on Facebook except you. It will take some time, sweat equity and some cash for advertising, but can you imagine the influence you could grow by simply being the administrator of a group this size?

The key is to make your page about the community not about your real estate business. You could place to links to your local business podcast, talk about community news, and allow other people in the community to interact.

Most people will not do this because it takes some time to build, but here is the reality…

**<u>Building a business is hard. Staying broke is hard. Choose your hard</u>.**

What could you build a community around? Is it a suburb? A city?

MAKE IT EASY TO DO BUSINESS WITH YOU AND OFFER A GUARANTEE

BuildYourBrandNow

The simple rule of business is this…make it easy to do business with you. I recently visited a department store to look for tee shirts. The rack was so full of shirts that I could not slide them enough to see the different designs. Within a few minutes, I decided it was too hard, so I moved on. They lost a sale. You don't want that to happen to your business. Ask yourself these questions…

Is it easy to find you? Do you return calls promptly? Do you have a communication system that will keep them informed? Are you utilizing technology to make signing documents easy?

I was constantly evaluating our business and asking if there were more efficient ways to serve our clients. How do we make their life easier? People are short on time and looking for fast results. Make it easy for them.

People also do not want to make a poor decision. When trying to choose an agent, they certainly don't want to make a wrong decision. By offering a guarantee, you will put their mind at ease. Maybe your guarantee is they can exit the contract if they are not happy for any reason.

Regardless of what guarantee you offer, make sure you honor it and that it doesn't contain a bunch of small print in order to qualify. In other words, if you say it mean it, even if it cost you money. You can earn more money: you can't always re-earn a stellar reputation.

BUILD YOUR TEAM OF TRUSTED VENDOR PARTNERS

BuildYourBrandNow

Building a team of trusted advisors is taking a page from the Dave Ramsey playbook. If you have ever listened to his radio show, He talks about his ELP's. That stands for Endorsed Local Providers. Dave positioned himself as an influencer on the radio, by speaking and through books as the advocate for people in debt. The more content he published, the higher his influence became. His audience takes his endorsements seriously. When Dave mentions an ELP, his listeners respond.

You can do the same in your business. The book, The Art of War, says that when you are small, you must appear big and significant. Having a team of endorsed providers makes you appear big. Don't hesitate…right now is your time to establish your team of approved vendors. Here is a list to get you started…

- Closing agent or attorney
- Loan Officer
- Home Inspector
- Insurance Agent
- Financial Planner
- Home Warranty Expert
- Home Repair Expert
- Roofer

Who else could you add to your growing list of endorsed providers?

CREATE LOCAL VIDEOS FEATURING YOU AS THE COMMUNITY REPORTER

BuildYourBrandNow

My friend and Real Estate Agent, Dale Erwin, lives in Fort Worth, Texas. We held a Personal Branding Mastery event for his real estate office in 2015. Dale admitted to me he was reluctant to attend because in his words… "he had seen it all." Dale stayed for the entire event and left with pages of notes. One of the strategies we discuss in the seminar is building your brand with video marketing.

Dale took that idea and ran with it. He now features local restaurants on his online TV show called Restaurants and Real Estate. What Dale is doing is leading with value first. He is celebrating the local restaurants in his video, which causes them to want to share his video out with their clients.

The equipment you will use is simple. Your smartphone and a "selfie stick" or another device to hold the phone. Eliminate your need to make your videos perfect. Remember, your job is to begin. You can perfect along the way.

Here are a couple of points to remember when doing video. First, make sure to hold your phone horizontal rather than vertical; doing so will cause the video to fill the post on social media. Second, upload your videos directly to Facebook and YouTube rather than posting the YouTube video link on Facebook.

What local businesses could you feature in your town? How would that drive up your visibility and referrals? How quickly could you begin?

# Want More? How Would You Like to Have a LIVE Personal Branding Mastery Seminar in Your City for FREE?

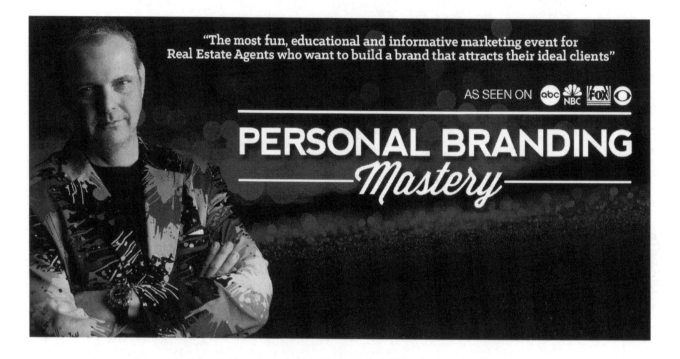

## To find out more about bringing Personal Branding Mastery to your city email Angie at
### Amdavis71@me.com

!

Awesome group of Agents in Raleigh NC at Personal Branding Mastery!

The house was packed with over 200 agents in New Jersey for Personal Branding Mastery

Always love sharing with Keller Williams – This was from Dallas Texas

Greensboro NC agents packed the house not once but twice for Personal Branding Mastery!

!

Minneapolis always has a welcoming crowd of agents for Personal Branding Mastery!

Atlanta showed up big time to learn branding!

More friends from the Personal Branding Mastery events!

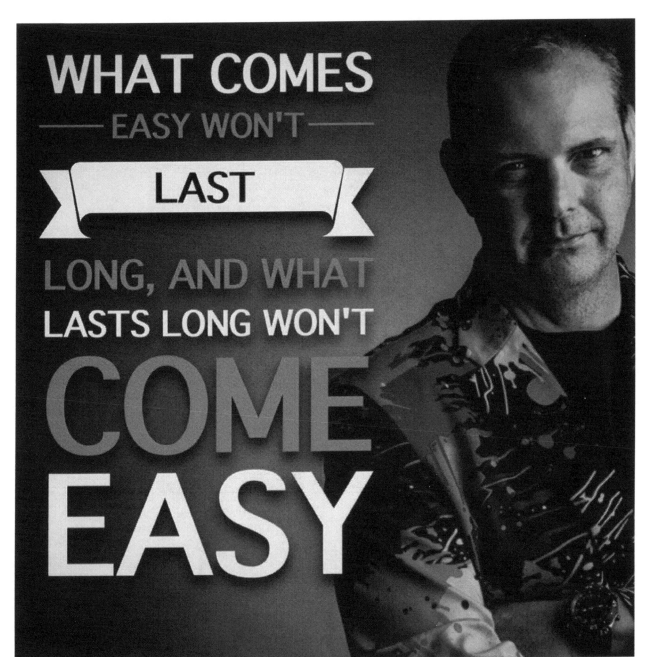

## ABOUT THE AUTHOR

Tim Davis is a believer in people, wearer of crazy socks, hopeless Dallas Cowboy fan and hacker of golf courses. He lives in Nashville, TN with his wife, Angie Davis and two cocker spaniels, Sheldon and Petey and the marketing dog, Landry. Growing up his family struggled financially and at 16 years old he took a job as a stock clerk at the local grocery store just to put food on the table. At the job interview the owner shared some advice that helped Tim not only escape the projects, but to graduate college, open his own mortgage company and speak on the same stage as Tony Robbins. That advice…always give more value then you receive. If you work hard on yourself and increase the value you bring, the market will reward you with business.

OBSERVE OTHERS BUT NEVER COMPARE YOUR START TO ANOTHER'S FINISH

BuildYourBrandNow

# Connect with Tim

timdavisonline@me.com

https://www.facebook.com/timwdavis

https://www.facebook.com/PersonalBrandMastery/

https://twitter.com/mtgevangelist

https://instagram.com/themarketingevangelist/

https://www.linkedin.com/in/timdavisonline

https://www.youtube.com/user/MKTGevangelist

https://www.TheMarketingEvangelist.com

Made in the USA
San Bernardino, CA
25 February 2020